Forbidden Tears

Stories, Poems & Essays of Trauma
from The Imprisoned Voices of
Unapologetic Black Youth

**Youth of Detroit Collegiate High
School**

Forbidden Tears
Copyright 2018 by **Detroit Collegiate High School**

ISBN: 978-1984909411

Detroit, Michigan 48207

Cover Art - **Ernell Ware**
Book Design & Editor - **Earneasha Byars**
Editor & English Teacher - **Sirrita Darby**

www.detroitcollegiate.org
www.eqeducation.org

Dedication

For those black and brown kids who continue to suffer in silence.

"Part of what makes a situation traumatic is not talking about it. Talking reduces trauma symptoms. When we don't talk about trauma, we remain emotionally illiterate. Our most powerful feelings go unnamed and unspoken." - *Tian Dayton*

"You're not a victim for sharing your story. You are a survivor setting the world on fire with your truth. And you never know who needs your light, your warmth, and raging courage." - *Alex Elle*

"Every African-American I know has two faces. There's the face that we have for ourselves and the face we put on for white America for the places we have to get to." - *Lee Daniels*

"This is what healing from trauma feels like: you are holding a dam together with superglue and behind it is a giant ocean of pain and all you have is this is superglue for the cracks in the cement. The trickles of pain through those cracks are enough to terrify you, but everyone around you seems oblivious, thinking, well you look like you're holding it together, you look like you're healing…so you must be fine." - *Nikita Gill*

Featured Authors

The following students have attended class healing sessions where they spoke about their pain and wrote their stories. They agreed to have them published in this book in hopes of helping others heal from their trauma as well. The work you see in this book is original work (revised and edited) of their stories and thoughts on trauma.

Micah Barnes
Diamand Batiste
Da'Juan Belk
Dante Belk
Janelle Boyles
Chawn Brown
Isis Brown
Earneasha Byars
Darnasha Cooper
Brianna Donald
Makayla Epps
Sankeya Forrest
Dekayla Fuggerson
Alex Hailey
Alexis Hailey
Jayla Harshaw
La'Ronte Hill

Kandise Hooks
Leondre Houston
Tatiana Ivey
Cora Jarrell
Diamond Jelks
Derrick Jones
Michael Jones
Alayzia Kendrick
Quiana Kyles
Iesha Leggett
Samuel Little
Mercedes Lucious
Mariah Mangum
Heavon Mapp
Darryl McGhee
China Miller
Ericka Minor
Cher'maine Moreland
Lenardo Moss
Caleb Paul
Mya Percy
Ralon Shobe
Shannon Siggers
Deshawn Smith
Kobi Sparks
Shantayshia Starks
Mikeal Threatt
Eleonna Ware
Quentez Whites

"Trauma is personal. It does not disappear if it is not validated. When it is ignored or invalidated the silent screams continue internally heard only by the one held captive. When someone enters the pain and hears the screams healing can begin."
- Danielle Bernock

Dying with Their Eyes Open
Foreword

Zora Neale Hurston said: "If you are silent about your pain, they will kill you and say you enjoyed it." It was my second year of teaching, and a usually perky and upbeat student showed up to my classroom that particular day desolate and melancholy. As I questioned her disposition, she proceeded to tell me that her brother got shot over the weekend and was in critical condition. Yet, this courageous soul still showed up to my classroom Monday morning. Although not as her full self, she was still there carrying that trauma on her back, and I realized that I was the first responder. How was I going to help her through this? How would this trauma virtually change the way this beautiful black girl navigated the rest of her life? What was more important that day, my finely curated lesson on text structures or that child's healing?

This particular incident and many others like it changed my whole philosophy of teaching and is the exact reason why I was lead in purpose to develop this book with my students. Children who experience trauma often have trouble in the classroom because their trauma can manifest itself as behavior issues, and my specific students seem to wake up to trauma like it's breakfast. They have become desensitized to such trauma because violence has become normalized in their communities. Most of my kids are suffering but since their suffering is invisible, it can be misinterpreted as something different. We spew inanities about what black kids need or how they should act but we rarely take the time to analyze the factors that contributed to that child's identity. We simply cannot underestimate the influence of trauma on the lives of our students.

I have switched my lens to look at all behavior issues for what they may be- combative acts that are a direct response to trauma. What teachers and administrators must realize is that all trauma is brought to schools. So why is it that everyone in the district can agree that addressing student trauma is important but we are still not urgent in making sure we get those trauma counselors in our schools because of the price-tag they come with? This is violence, enacted on a much subtler but potentially far more dangerous level.

When students are traumatized, teachers are too. When my kids are suffering, so am I!

Understanding these factors gave me a charge that birthed "Forbidden Tears." Writing for their healing has served as an opportunity for my students to use their words to bring power to their realities. Systems of oppression that harvest trauma have not allowed my students to show up to my classroom as their full selves. So, we must amplify the voices of those kids who have been walking and growing in a world that has sought to silence their pain. I remember growing up when I would cry about things that my parents saw as miniscule, their typical response would always be, "Why are you crying...I'll give you something to cry about!" Let's face it - black kids aren't allowed to show any type of emotion regarding pain, period, and God forbid our suffering turns to tears shed.

For the purpose of healing, I created a safer space for my kids because I honestly believe there is no such thing as a "safe space" for students of color in schools. I knew that only when my students' voices were heard deep learning and even deeper healing could truly happen. However, I also understood that my students have built their whole identities around the trauma they grew up with so when I offered support in the form of storytelling, many rejected the help, because they are so hurt, so broken, so traumatized that they didn't trust it. My kids do not need a savior. They simply need to be taught by someone with true passion and conviction ready to give them the tools they need to break down barriers and change the cycle in their communities. So, for everyone who reads this, I leave you with a charge to no longer fail those students who we clearly see dying with their eyes open.

-Sirrita Darby, 2018
Social Justice Educator

J'm Afraid
Earneasha Byars

I'm afraid that one day I'll go to school, then
never leave. Gunshots will go off and I'll
forever bleed. I'm Afraid that because I'm
black, my dreams will never be freed. They'll
stay underground like an unsprouted seed. It's
safe to say our future isn't promised. With
global warming steady increasing around us. I
wonder if North Korea still trying to bomb us?
As a whole, we kill each other every day. If it
could be prevented before, how come
afterwards we pray? While the incarceration
rate is becoming abrupt, we still have people in
the "hood" throwing gang signs up. Schools
nowadays are terrible and if my family got that
call, it would be unbearable. Do we even learn?
Well, I guess that's none of your concern. If
you saw them in flames, I bet you'd let them
burn. I'm Afraid and you should know. These
fears haunt and taunt me but I don't let them
show. But since I shared them with you, would
you help or would you let them grow?

A World Without Racism
Diamand Batiste

Can you imagine a world without racism? I bet you can't, especially in society today. But honestly with time and effort this could change. Of course, this seems ridiculous and impossible. However, it's always good to try. Also, the best way to make something happen is to start with you. Again, this isn't going to happen overnight, so I came up with three steps to get this society started.

First and foremost, love yourself. I know this may sound a little odd but this is actually very beneficial. You cannot learn to love others without first loving yourself. Every day when you awake, look into the mirror and say, "I am beautiful/handsome" or "I have purpose." The more that you say it, the more you'll believe it. Once you learn to love yourself, you'll be able to start loving others, which leads us to the next step.

Learn to love others. Pick up a book and read about people of different races. Learning their history is the best way to start. One, not only are you educating yourself but two, you'll be open-minded to other cultures. If you're in school, ask questions, don't be afraid to get all of the information that you may need. After you learn about them, you're ready for the final step.

Social interactions. Now I know what you may be thinking, social interactions? Yes, now is your time to actually communicate. If they aren't so kind in return then at least you did something good and this is a great way to make more friends. Just a simple, "Hello" or "Good Afternoon" could start an amazing friendship. Most importantly, this could end a lot of racism in the world. This will most likely take time but it'll all be worth it in the end.

With these steps, I feel we can eliminate racism. Though a lot of people won't actually try, it's good to get as many people as we can to start. Now let's go create a world without racism.

Better Than That
Shannon Siggers

I just don't understand how every man is free if
we are not. They want to beat us down every
time we try to get up. They say we're the beast
but they are the true animals behind the mask.
They kill us because they don't understand us. I
don't even know who to trust. Don't give them
a reason to spill my blood in these streets. Will
it even help if they pull their pants up? Do I
have to bleach my skin to be free? My skin is
beautiful. Black is beautiful. Do you think I'm
done? Were you done when hundreds of people
who look like me were whipped and lynched?
They say we're thugs and our emotions are only
seen as anger. No matter what we become
stronger, wiser and better than what they said
we would be.

No Matter What Black Child
Tatiana Ivey

God created you equal, no matter what that
white man tells you.
You're not a disgrace to your community, no
matter what the news publicizes.
You only smoke because your family doesn't
listen to you, no matter what statistics say.
I know you only sell weed to help your family
out, no matter what the cops say.
We know you're suffering from depression, no
matter what your mom says.
We know you're not okay, no matter what the
therapist says.
Come on nah, you know you don't feel smart
enough and that's your reason for being a class
clown.
You know you use sports to get your mind off
of things, no matter how loud the coach yells.
Embrace the feeling of being a black child,
THEY DON'T understand, no matter what they
say, THEY JUST DON'T understand.

Home-wrecked
Jayla Harshaw

Let me introduce you all to a little girl named
Jayla. She grew up without her father, until the
age of 13. Her momma and daddy would fight
and hurt each other, until Jayla came. Put in
your mind that Jayla's daddy had 4 other kids
besides Jayla by other women. Jayla's daddy
did nothing for her. He didn't spend time with
her. He wouldn't even call and check to see if
she was okay. When Jayla was 5 years old, her
momma and daddy were arguing. Her daddy
was outside while Jayla and her momma was
inside. They were yelling through windows and
she wouldn't let him come get Jayla. And all
you can hear is Jayla screaming and yelling, "I
want my daddy!" So after that night everything
was over and done with. A few years later Jayla
was turning 13 years old, mind you Jayla's
daddy didn't call or didn't even come see her
until now when she turned 13. Her daddy was
getting married and she was going to be in the
wedding. Then her dad's mom started lying.
She lied and said that Jayla didn't want to be in

the wedding. So her daddy didn't call to make sure that's what she said or anything. The day of the wedding came and Jayla got home before her momma. Jayla was crying and her momma found her and knew the day of the wedding was today, so she called her daddy and started cussing him out. It made her mad, Jayla stopped calling her daddy and asking for stuff because he never did anything for her. Jayla thought it was just one less kid out of 5 that he didn't have to worry about. But long story short, Jayla was very hurt and just wanted to have that father figure, and wants to have that bond that every little girl has with their dad. So she felt like her home was wrecked because she didn't have both of her parents with her. She just wanted love from her daddy. He started doing better but it still didn't feel the same because she didn't have that bond with him to begin with.

Killed by The System
Samuel Little

I believe the system is against us. The system in real life is designed against us due to the things that have happened to black people. For example, innocent black men killed by the system mentally or physically due to things they didn't do. There is a long list of examples of innocent black people killed because of our skin color.

Discrimination in the justice system can be seen each and every day. For example, discrimination in the court system. An example would be the Kalief Browder documentary. Kalief was at Rikers Island for three years. He was wrongly accused of stealing a backpack. Kalief was beat and mentally abused because they felt he was the weakest link. One of those three years Kalief was in solitary confinement.

Discrimination has been going on for over 100 years. Slavery is another example of racism. Racism can be seen every day with police officers, judges, and juries. Innocent black people like Trayvon Martin, Kalief

Browder, Emmett Till, and Martin Luther King died because of racism.

Racism is a synonym for discrimination. People have been protesting for equality for so many years, too many years. Black people have been mistreated for the longest. The system is undoubtedly against us because of our skin color and it will probably continue because of what people are taught in their home or what people grow up believing. Something's gotta give.

Never Knew Racism Until I Came Here?
Lenardo Moss

I never knew what racism was until I moved to the United States. Where I'm from black people are the majority. Not saying life is perfect there. But back in the Bahamas, I didn't have to worry about being a target because of my color. I did not have to worry about which street to hang out on and how late. I physically learned what racism was while moving to the United States.

Being black in the United States makes you an automatic target. Being a black male makes you an even bigger one. It could cost you your life here. They don't care who you are. Just know if you're black your life doesn't matter to them. Police brutality is terrible, they shoot you like bottles on a wall.

Young black men become targets here. They want us gone. We have to be careful of the clothes we wear, the music we listen to and how we wear our hair. These examples are how stereotypes are used against us. We see these things as fashion, they see them as threats.

If I have an afro, wear a hoodie, and sag my pants, I am now a target. I'm looked at as if I'm a criminal. They don't see me looking decent like I do. They see me as trouble-maker. I'm not even allowed to express myself without without being judged.

Moving to the United States has taught me first-hand about discrimination. I never hated the police. I never felt that the color of my skin mattered until now. My grandfather worked with the police force. Because of that, I'm more careful about what I do or where I go. Because of racism I am a young black target. Every single day.

Two-Faced
Earneasha Byars

Detroit, where you might become brave.
Detroit, where you might end up in a grave.
The place where new things uprise,
Then are brought down with surprise.
Boom, shots fired. The police release two.
One suspect move then they're done with you.
This city's slowly moving under,
Like they've been struck by lightning or
thunder.

Don't get me wrong, my city's beautiful.
Science Center, DIA, Charles Wright, are all
very useful.
The art, the music, and cultural ways,
Detroit, where I spend most of my days.
Big on cars and manufacturing,
Activists, advocates, steady lecturing.
My city's on a come up,
If you don't agree, you can honestly shut up.

Two-faced Detroit, with our two-faced ways,
This is the place where Motor City lays.

A City that Cries
Shannon Siggers

Detroit is my city you should know it's also
known as Motor City.
A city filled with diversity.
A place where boys think they're men if they
carry a gun.
Where they commit crimes just for fun.
A place that had one of the biggest riots.
Where they sell drugs but try to hide it.
Where when someone white dies it's a crisis.
Where when someone black dies people
become biased.
If someone sees something wrong, they remain
silent.
If you think Detroit is all bad you need some
clarity.
Detroit has some good for example, when they
give to charities.
Detroit has many accomplishments and many
establishments.
Detroit has museums including Charles Wright,
Henry Ford, Institute of Arts, only to name a
few.

Detroit is increasing in sizing, so you should be here for its uprising.

"Doesn't matter how tough we are, trauma always leaves a scar. It follows us home, it changes our lives, trauma messes everybody up, but maybe that's the point. All the pain and the fear and the crap. Maybe going through all of that is what keeps us moving forward. It's what pushes us. Maybe we have to get a little messed up, before we can step up."

- Alex Karev

Look at Me
Kandise Hooks

Look at me.
    Tell me what you see.
    A black girl with nappy hair?
    Do you think I'm beautiful?
    Do you care?
Look at me.
    Tell me what you see.
    Will you judge me by my cover,
    Or flip through my pages and see what
    you discover.
Look at me.
    Tell me what you see.
    Will you judge me by what you know or
    WHAT YOU THINK?

DETROIT: The Anomaly
Cher'Maine Moreland

Detroit is my city,
You should know Motor City lies here.
When we hear a gunshot,
And run away with fear.
When the government hears my cries,
But they just cover their ears.

Detroit is my city and I'm proud to say it.
Where my kind stands up and the police hates
it.
Where young black men do whatever it takes,
Because it's never enough what they "mama"
make.

Detroit is my city,
And it is known for the violence.
But little do you know we are all angels,
Just in disguises.
When we scream the truth, when they say "stay
quiet"
When they get nervous cause my people are not
hiding.

Detroit is my city
And I'm saying it loud.
So I do what I can to make my city proud.

Puzzle Pieces
Brianna Donald

I left at 4:30, "Be back by 10!" Hair half done,
but I'm with my friend. Hat covers my head,
black tank top and blue pants. A football game,
laughs and fun. Game over, our team won! Out
to eat, then a familiar place with smiles
plastered on my face. Prank calls and videos are
what we get into. Telling corny jokes and
making up dances make our personalities
collide with joy. Almost over, time to get going.
Roads are bumpy but we don't mind, we're
having fun of all kinds. Then "POP!" We stop,
the lights go black. Cries and sadness flood
through like a waterfall. Confusion is all I feel
and smoke is all I smell. "It's okay, we're
okay," I tell myself, but we're not. My mom's
number? I don't remember. I'm hurting, it hurts.
Hat fell off my head, black tank top and blue
blood covered pants. Panic now is all I feel.
Hospital lights blind me, police ask me
questions I don't want to answer. CPS blocks
my mom from coming to see me. The doctors
say fragments, but I say puzzle pieces, pieces

that make me. Not indestructible but strong. I left at 4:30, never got back by 10. She doesn't always say it, but my mom blames me, so much that I blame me too. Even though she says she doesn't, I know her too well, but I push through that feeling even though it feels like hell. So I take my puzzle pieces as you can see, and try my very best to put back together me.

Life is Strange
Michael Jones

I feel like racism is bad and it's been going on for way too long. When you're black, you're labeled as a thief, drug dealer, and all kinds of bad stuff. Even white policemen will shoot you because you're black! You move, they beat you. Reach for license and registration, they shoot you. It's not right, everyone has rights and you should know them. If you heard of Tupac, he stood up for what was right. He didn't want black people to go to jail or get treated wrong. For example, the movie "All Eyez on Me." In the movie, Tupac saw a black man was getting treated bad and Tupac did something. He went in the car and got his gun out and shot at the white man. That was bad but he felt like it was wrong for the treatment they gave the black man. I had to deal with that type of stuff when I moved to a city called Port Huron. I went to Central which is a a middle school and this boy he was arguing with my friend Daquan and I got in the middle of it and tried to break it up. The only thing I said was, "Yall need to stop, it's not that big of a deal" and then the boy said "shut the fuck up you nigger" out loud so me and Daquan got mad and was about to fight the boy because he had no reason to say that. So, we started fighting and me and Daquan got suspended but the boy didn't. I think it was because we were some of the few blacks at an all-white school. I regret it but still know your rights and stand up for yourself no matter what.

Unaccepted
DaJuan Belk

All the things going on in yo home and you feel
all alone.
The police they killed Khalil, they put a bullet
in his dome.
Put a bullet in his head, he was laying there
dead.
Now his mom and his grandma laying in bed
just crying
and the police they're lying.
Who can you trust if you can't trust the ones
who's supposed to protect and serve?
If you killed and don't get locked up you'll get
what you deserve.
It's his word over a dead boy.
People wondering what's going through his
head boy.
But he ain't do nothing to be dead boy.
Besides get his mom back right
You gotta do what you gotta do to get yo family
tight.
You having yo daddy lying for you
and just crying for you.

Like the people owe you, making it seem like
it's right that he died.
But these the type of things that make black
people strive.

The Life of a Black Male Rising
Caleb Paul

Once upon a time, a king was born on
November 6, 2002. His name was Caleb Paul.
He was a different kid. When all the other kids
went outside and played with their friends, he
didn't. He stayed in the house and watched TV.
Other kids were mean to him, they called him
names and made fun of him because he stutters.
He felt bad about himself and didn't want to go
to school. Weeks passed by and he finally
decided to go to school. The next day had begun
and he was nervous. So he got up and got
dressed and finally got in the car. On the way to
school he was quiet the whole time. He walked
in the school sweating, as he walked to class
and paused outside the door, the flashbacks
began. Playing over and over in his head. He
snapped back into reality and he remembered
what his mom always told him, "Stop and take
a deep breath." So he stopped and took a deep
breath. He started thinking and believing that if
he does this then words couldn't hurt him. He is
somebody! After that, he never cared about

what other people had to say about him.
Nobody's perfect in this cold place we call
Earth.

Born In The Hood
Chawn Brown

Everyone knows that the hood is a very
dangerous place for the people in it. It's filled
with poor people and a couple of rich drug
dealers. Most people in the hood don't really
expect anything from anyone because they're
probably just as poor or have the same
problems. Kids all around are in their emotions
because they can't afford what they want or
better yet, what they need. Dads are rarely
around and don't want to see their kids. People
in the hood depend mostly on government
assistance like welfare and bridge cards. They
need help putting clothes and food on the table
every month for their families. Plenty of crimes
happen in the hood like robberies and murders.
There is a huge drug population in these
selective areas. Everyone gets hooked on it
because they see it. That's how the hood is.
Hopefully it'll change some day or the hood is
forever just going to be "The Hood."

The White Man's Thoughts
Alayzia Kendrick

Blacks are useless.
Blacks are a harm to society.
Blacks are a groups of animals.
Blacks are not equal to me.
Blacks are made to be separated.
Blacks are meant to be slaves.
Blacks harm everyone.
Blacks are criminals.
Blacks are thieves.
Blacks skin is too dark.
Blacks are broke.
Blacks are ugly.
Blacks are dumb.

Black people are not equal to us and never will be.

They will never go anywhere but to jail or a grave sight.

The Black Community
Ralon Shobe

Most black men that are born in Detroit are
born into a society where they are already a
target. By the time most black men get to the
eleventh grade they're thinking about dropping
out. College is the last thing on their mind,
survival is the first. It's sad, but that's how it is
today. A good percent of us (black men or black
people in general) excel on tests like SAT,
ACT, or NWEA. Some people might assume
differently because we're black. It's just
stereotypes that they expect black people to live
up to.
Every black child is not without a father. Or all
black parents aren't on drugs or doped out. In
my experience, I've seen some black
communities like this but to put the label on all
of us just isn't right. In my opinion, being
"Black" puts a list of automatic stereotypes on
our backs and we must prove all those people
wrong.

"Until the legacy of remembered and reenacted trauma is taken seriously, black America cannot heal."

- bell hooks

A Country Divided; A World Divided Forever
Earneasha Byars

We live in a world that's changing constantly
because we're not taking care of our planet
responsibly.
There's Republicans in office trying to run us
out supposedly and we're not fulfilling the
duties we're supposed to be.
We have one life, one Earth.
The planet where we supply birth.
To be separated by something as silly as race.
Climate change seems to be picking up it's
pace.
Wake up, Wake up America!
If you haven't noticed, everyone else is trying
to get ahead of us.
We rap and sing about how much we really "got
it."
But what ever happened to helping the ones
without it?
We walk in and out of school without actually
learning.

Yet we let the ones in charge take home their
earnings.
We let the fairer skin tell us we're ghetto and
ratchet.
Opinionated or fact-ed, man this world is hectic.
I'm not preaching or taking you to school but if
you don't wake up this precious Earth will be
gone because of you fools.
I'm not worried about if you are Hispanic, you
could be Muslim if you want.
I don't discriminate against Whites and I don't
care what Asians look like.
Believe it or not, but it's actually true
You need to wake up because this world's
future is counting on you.

All My Life
Kobi Sparks

All my life I was by myself.
All my life I had to do everything by myself.
All my life I had to figure out what was right
and what was wrong.
All my life I had to break the rules for reasons
unknown.
All my life I had to eat syrup sandwiches.
All my life I went to sleep hungry.
All my life I had to help feed my family.
All my life I had to wait until the holidays to eat
a real meal.
All my life I had to wait for everything.
All my life I had to struggle.
All My Life.

Warren Days
Mikeal Threatt

Back to the Warren days, where bad luck pays.
Homies robbing Homies, getting put inside a
grave.
Steady hitting licks, girls getting treated like
maids.
I was just chillin', tryna stay back, pops got
jumped and hit with a strap.
I was really hurt, friends out to lurk.
I watched another man put his killer in the dirt.
Grew up without my pops, tryna get some
money getting back on top.
Fam feelings came out, I saw they real eyes.
People gave up on me, felt like I was paralyzed.
But at the end of the day, guess what?
I'm going high.

From Tragedy to Reflection
Quiana Kyles

When I was 7 years old, all I used to hear was "She's not your real mom, stop calling her that!" I never believed it because I stayed with her. I used to argue my nephews up and down that she was my actual mom. I figured that she was because she bought me clothes and always gave me extra money when I needed/wanted it. When I turned 12, my mom sat me down and explained to me that she was not my birth mom. She explained that I was adopted and my real mother was her cousin. Her name was Lucy. I never understood why she lied to me. She could've told me that when I used to fight with my nieces and nephews about her being my mom. When she told me that I was adopted she went into deep details about why. My real mom made the wrong choices when she was young and it followed her. Like doing drugs, being addicted, and not being able to take care of her child. As she explained it more, she made sure to include the fact that my real mom loved me and did what was best for me.

In 2013, when my sister died, I met my birth mother. It was December 30th at my sister's funeral. A few years later, my real parents started coming around. I started to catch on a little more. When I was little, I used to have seizures. I didn't even know that it was because of her drug addiction. Eventually, I started to blame my sister's death on her because she died from brain injuries. After I saw that they didn't plan on being in my life the question of, "Living with them," went down the drain. In 2016, I started to question myself again when I got jumped at Osborn High School. I never went back to school. I started to ask myself that if I lived with my real mom, would I be in my correct grade? Would I be able to go school and succeed? I didn't want to leave my so-called mom, but I really wanted things to be right. I asked my birth mom one day if it would be possible and she told me no. After that, I just started to fall back. I probably wasn't going to leave my so-called mom anyways, after all I am her caregiver. I wasn't thinking at the time, I just wanted what was best for me. Now here I am taking care of my so-called mom and I'm in school catching up on my credits, doing well though. My so-called mom is a huge blessing to me. If it wasn't for her, I wouldn't be who I am today. I actually learned from my situation because when I grow up I want to work in a girls home. I want my story to go viral because it's a lot of people who was put up for adoption and probably feel how I feel. When I first found out that my mother was addicted to drugs I was furious but I learned that sometimes you can't help it. I want to give some girls the therapy that I didn't have. Now it's 2018 and I still try to communicate with my parents but I haven't talked to them in weeks. I still love them because I know if they would have kept me then I would've been in a bad situation so they really did do what was best for me. From Tragedy to Growth.

The Perception of Me
Diamand Batiste

Perception is key but perception can also be the death of me. The second I am born, I'm already brought into a society that is ready to bring me down, instead of rising me up. Especially since I am a black woman, my emotions are seen as anger. My kids in the future will be seen as a way to get government revenue. But wait... that's just how you perceive me.

You don't know me, the kind, ambitious, intelligent, passionate, determined, humble me. You don't know the struggle I have to be put through to make a living in this society. I have to work twice as hard than you do just to barely get by. I have to be patient because my responses aren't valid. I have to work hard to earn respect while yours is just handed right to you.

Perception is everything, perception is a way of regarding, understanding, or interpreting something or someone. With that being said, why does the actions of others define me? I am my own person, so do not compare me to the people who are ignorant. I am only responsible for what I say, not for what you understand. Perception may be key, but what matters the most is how you see yourself.

The Worst Disappearing Act
Derrick Jones

Where to start? Well, I'm an African American
student in Detroit. I grew up without a mother.
Maybe that's why my personality is so dry. My
mother, well what can I say, tried to change her
ways. That didn't go too well. When she let us
know, actually our grammy told us (she lived
down the street from our grammy). We went to
her then ended up spending the night. After that
weekend, her, our sisters, and brothers moved
and we haven't heard from them since. I guess it
was occasional that we'd hear from her. It
saddens me how people can just leave their
kids. Like how can you live with yourself
knowing you left two of your kids? How can
you have kids if you're just going to leave them
without a mother? It's wrong for people to be
like that. I'm 15 now, with two brothers and a
dad I live with and I am going to be okay.

Stereotypes
Dekayla Fuggerson

I am a black child who believes I can do
anything I put my mind to. I believe I am smart,
but not everybody thinks that. I'm black so I
might not be smart. I'm black so I don't care
about my education. I'm a young black female
so when I get older I am supposed to be a maid.
I'm only capable of cooking and cleaning. I am
a black female, but why should I be defined by
my ethnicity or race. I am black and smart. All
black boys sag their pants or are in gangs. Will
them pulling their pants up change what you
think about them? Nobody says anything about
white men that sag. Pretty girls aren't smart.
Why can't pretty girls be smart? I know pretty
girls who are smart and care about their
education. Different races like whites may think
we are nasty or bad people, when we really
aren't bad people at all.

My Lifeline Goals
Darryl McGhee

My lifeline story involves my education, reaching goals, being the best I can be, and also striving to meet my goals. There was a time where I didn't think that I'd make it this far. Things I could imagine like keeping a high GPA in school. I remember the times I would always get suspended from school and come home unsatisfied. I can also remember the times I'd throw away my homework before I went home. I wanted better for myself so I had to stand up for myself and start over.

You Live by The Choices You Make

Mercedes Lucious

"You Live By The Choices You Make" was all I heard growing up as a kid. Growing up as a kid was hard for me. Growing up in a neighborhood full of drugs and abandoned houses. Growing up as a young black girl was even harder. All I heard as a little kid was "awe she black" and "awe she not gone amount to anything." My parents, grandparents, and other siblings always told me "awe don't worry about them, they just talking." But I had no other choice but to worry about it or pay attention to it if I hear it almost every day. As a child, I wondered why they are saying these things or why are they treating people differently? That's when I finally learned about racism, but it still didn't make sense to me. Really? People treat other people different because of the color of their skin? That's very ignorant to me. I always wondered why my teachers always treated some students differently but hey that's the type of world we living in and it is a disgrace. So I shouldn't be surprised with what I'm going through. It's so crazy to see my brothers and sisters in this world being drug dealers and selling their bodies on the corner when they can be lawyers and doctors. My grandmother always told me "you can make an example out of this world" or "you can be the one to change this world" and I believe in that. So here I stand today saying, "You live by the choices you make so make the best ones!"

Hello, Are You Here?
Darnasha Cooper

This young lady was 14, her name was Darnasha. Throughout her 14 years of life, she's been through a lot. When she was just 2 years old she met her father. He was perfect and fitted just right in her life. He would wake her up everyday, take care of her, take her to school and everything. When she turned 5, a tall strange man came into her life and said he was her father. She didn't believe it, so she went about her day. That next week, she had to take a test. Her mommy told her the strange man was her father, it hurt her dearly because she's been living a lie. She was the only child on her father side or whoever the strange man was. She went to spend the night with the man she didn't know. He used to beat her for not speaking, beat her for not eating, and beat her for not listening. But little did he know, she was confused, she didn't know him. He left and never came back, missed everything and he didn't come back until she turned 13. First day of kindergarten graduation, award ceremonies, yeah, he missed everything. Her stepfather was there for it all though, but then he stopped caring. She use to have emotional breakdowns. Her mommy use to try to calm her down because her attitude use to have her crazy. But she was not crazy, just a girl trying to find herself in this world.

In My Life
La'Ronte Hill

In my life I've been through a lot of things. I grew up without a father. I was in a gang and I remember a person following me. We ended up fighting that person because he was in a different gang. I shoot at that person 3 times and Thank God, I missed all 3 times. I remember in middle school, I got jumped at Denby Park. To this day, I don't like school because of the students at the school. I didn't care much in 9th grade. I passed with a 1.9 GPA. I can remember my step dad beating on my mom. He had a field day whenever he would beat her. I remember my mom calling the police every day on my step dad.

I got to a point where I wanted to kill that person and I don't know what stopped me from killing that person. I lived through that even though I was going through hell. Because of his actions, my mom threw him out and to this day I haven't seen him. Police was asking a lot of questions about my step-dad and I got tired of all of it. After this Denby put me out of they school when it was like 12 days of school left. I remember growing up on 7 mile. I played football for the West Seven Rams, Running Back number 7. I was the fastest on the team and scored 27 touchdowns in my PAL season. I went crazy. Now I'm in the 10th and I'm going to play football for Detroit Collegiate. I want to be in the NFL and I want to be a Running Back and I want to get my family off the streets and get them somewhere safe. Period.

A Million Dimes
Heavon Mapp

I was always in the wrong, always sung a sad
song.
Chosen more than golden.
The one she was always scolding.
Just wanted her attention and love.
Wish an angel was sent from above.
My grandma showed tough love.
Treated me like a thug.
Something like a beef.
Never left me in the streets.
I was different from the rest.
I figured she loved me the best.
Just had a hard way of showing it.
A lot of chances I was blowing it.
She got sick and was in the hospital.
I was so hurt, heart melted like a popsicle.
Came in and she couldn't open her eyes.
But when I came in it was a surprise.
She opened her eyes really wide.
I really prayed to God.
Then in like a month she died.
I cried and cried.

They said they did their job, the doctors really lied.
My love for her is nationwide.
At your funeral I went crazy.
God, why did you take my baby?
Just yesterday I was in thought.
That's when the first tear was caught.
You're the reason I'm doing good.
Raised me up out the hood.
Wish I could repay you for your time.
Your life and spirit was worth a million dimes.

There's no one to tell and nowhere to hide. I kept the pain to myself while a part of me died.

Hard Times But Better Days
Quentez Whites

Detroit born and raised was rough for me. Just looking back at when I was younger and how I'm in a better place now. When I was younger, my mom really didn't have much because growing up as a single parent with my dad being locked up from being a drug dealer was hard for her. Especially with raising three boys. But she always made sure we had a roof over our head and food on the table. My oldest brother always was in some trouble by fighting and getting kicked out of school. My mom use to drink a lot to relieve some of her stress and she gambled a lot as well. Her ex-boyfriend use to beat on us and her. But then we moved to the westside when our house got shot up. But moved back to the eastside about a year later when my brother ended up getting shot in his neck beefing with someone over some petty stuff. But he slowed down his ways because life is just too short. Then 2 years after that, my grandma died from breast cancer and that messed up the whole family because she was the one that kept us together. But then my mom realized that she's a strong woman and that she's a hard-working person and now she got a good job and she's taking care of us and I love and appreciate her so much for her sacrifices.

My Twin Passing
Shantayshia Starks

It started when her momma passed away. She was very sick. She was sick before but nobody told me anything. They claim I was too young to understand but I actually understood more than what they thought I did. So when her momma passed, I spent months with her. She wouldn't get out the bed, she would barely eat anything and she would sleep all day.

I would try to make her eat and I would stay in the room and watch her sleep. So after 3 months, I went home that summer when school started back and February rolled around. It was a afternoon and my big sister and cousins were over. My big sister was doing hair and my cousins was chilling doing they own thing. I was watching my sister do hair when my mom and auntie walked in the house. My momma ran up the stairs and slammed her door.

My auntie called me and my sister upstairs. When she called us up there she had tears in her eyes. Her eyes were red and puffy and she said she had some bad news. Then she said Domonique had died and my eyes started to water. I kept saying she was lying. I just could not believe it. Then the tears just rolled out and they wouldn't stop. I cried so hard.

Two days later, I went to school and everybody knew what happened. Everyone knew why I was so sad. One of my teachers told me to go to the school counselor. When I went to the school counselor, she asked me what was going on and I told her why I was sad. She told me to try to remember all the good times we had and how much of a good person she was.

Ever since then, my whole life changed and my attitude got worse. I started to get in trouble every day. I got suspended a lot and I kept fighting and got kicked out of school. My anger just got so bad. My mouth gets me in so much trouble and I tend to snap on people in a matter of seconds. My life just changed so much since Domonique and her momma passed. Life has been a living hell and it seems like it's going to get worse before it gets better.

Hopefully me, my sister and mother lives will get better in 2018. 2017 just hasn't been our year and sometimes I just don't wanna live anymore but I am here and I am continuing.

When I Was A Little Girl
Iesha Leggett

When I was little, a lot went on. My
mommy and daddy did a lot of arguing and my
daddy would walk out. I was little and clueless
and asked myself, "What if I grow up like
others without a father?" When my mama
would bathe me and put me to bed, I would not
even be sleep foreal. I would just lay there
thinking while my mama and daddy argued. My
dad always stayed the night at grandma's house.
He would come back looking all confused and
stuff looking for me but I wouldn't be there.
Both of my brothers went to jail for nonsense
that I still to this day don't know the real reason
why, I was 5 at the time. We kept moving and
we would stay in a place for a while before we
would move again. My second oldest sister
moved out when she was 18. She only moved
around the corner though. Her first born was a
girl named De'Zarah. She kinda had a hard time
with her because she was still young herself and
everyone would tell her that babies don't come
with instructions but I guess she didn't listen. I

was the one with all the questions like "Why our family can't be normal?" She be like "Our life was just set up different."

When I first started middle school, I didn't get along with people foreal so my mama would have to come to the school every other day. I had a few good friends. They were fun to hang out with in and out of school. Then my sister got pregnant again, this time a boy. She named him after his dad "Albert James Winn III." Then when she moved from around the corner, she moved all the way across town. She had a third baby and it was another girl, "Alaina Latrice Winn." When Alaina was born, they thought she had one kidney instead of two, then she had to get switched over to the children's hospital. She was there ever since she was born because of the breathing problems she was having. My niece turned three months and passed away because her heart rate dropped and she stopped breathing. Everyone was so hurt and I am so proud of my sister for being so strong for us and Alaina. Now I'm in high school. I'm still growing and forming so not everything they have expected me to go through has gotten to me yet. "Growing up, here I come."

I'm Black and Ain't Going Back
Alex Hailey

My meaning of Black and ain't going back is
like slavery.
Back then the whites had our ancestors working
in cotton fields all day.
They would tie us up and beat us to take their
anger away.
But now it's time to make a change.
We have a racist president, Donald Trump, in
the office.
What we got in the office now is a complete
loss, that will probably cause a nuclear
holocaust.
And while the drama pops and he waits for stuff
to quiet down, he'll just gas his plane up and fly
around until the bombing stops.
I'm Black and ain't going back also stands for
our future generations because just cause we are
Black don't mean Whites have to treat us as if
we are inferior.
I say I'm Black and ain't going back because it
really seems that Blacks still don't have their
natural rights in the Declaration Of

Independence.
I'M BLACK AND IM PROUD......(SAY IT
LOUD).

The Dynasty of China
China Miller

I am China and I am 14 years old, a
Detroiter, and my mom is the most important
person in my life. She was there for me
throughout my whole life even through the
difficult problems. My mom had me at 16 years
old and people always told her she's not going
to be nothing, I'm not going to be nothing, and
we both gone be a failure and a dropout and all
that. Now because of that, she's stronger than
ever. My momma had me before her own
birthday which is crazy. My mom is 31 years
old and is doing better than ever. But my dad is
not important to me at all. He's a nobody to me
and I do not care for him, not even a little.

When I was 4 years old, I had a party for
my birthday at my house and everyone came
and had fun. I told my sperm donor that I had a
"boyfriend" and he got really angry. He twisted
my arm and pushed me into the television. I
was crying and my momma came and asked me
what was wrong and I told her what happened
and that night they got into an argument and he

just stopped coming around completely. He calls my mom from time to time and be wanting to talk to me but I never wanna talk to him. When I was 10 or 11 years old, I was molested by a man I didn't even know. My parents didn't even know who he was either and I am still dealing with it today. All throughout school, I was always considered shorter than everyone and they started to think that I was weak. I'm not, I just don't argue with people cause it's pointless. This past year I witnessed death twice in 2 months. My uncle died. He was shot in the head and his body got cut up and they burnt the house up. He was basically my life and I miss him so much. My brother died by getting hit by a car. He was still breathing but the doctors gave him too much pressure so he died. Throughout my whole life I witnessed pain, hurt, and mixed emotions. But my story is my dynasty.

Nothing But The Real
Alexis Hailey

Roses are Red, Violets are Blue, Malcolm X
dead because of these fools.
You should be chillin but you rather be trippin.
If you not a blood then you must be crippin.
You in between but it's obvious you popping
sixes then you wonder why
the government don't deal with our district.
You got President Trump already starting his
mission.
But we really can't complain, we put ourselves
in this position.
Just really tired of everything I'm trying to
make a million.
Don't know what yall tryna do but I know I'm
about my business.
I come to school everyday cause I'm really try
to educate.
And when I'm gone don't show unreal love
cause I really don't have time for the phony and
the fake.
Have you ever heard the phrase "It's a cold
world, don't know what we gon make out of it."

Difficult times really but we can make it right.
We should come together like MLK did when
he was fighting for our rights.
Roses are red, Violets are blue, help us through
all battles cause that's what leaders do.

It Just Doesn't Make Sense
Earneasha Byars

It doesn't make sense how surprised people are to find out how smart I am. It doesn't make sense that because my vocabulary is so widespread, I must've grown up with white kids. Is it surprising that I know how to read and acquire knowledge? Why are you confused that I have intellectual endowment? Is it expected growing up a black woman, I'm supposed to be minimized by knowledge? It just doesn't make sense.

You'll be surprised at how many times I hear, "You're smart," on a daily basis. Sometimes being characterized like this frustrates me. It shows what society expects from me. I know they don't really want blacks to learn anything. Being a black woman makes it even harder. Am I only supposed to know how to take care of a household? Is it set up only for me to cook, clean, have children, and satisfy the man? Why don't they want me to write, learn what y-intercept is or how the Earth spins on its axis?

I don't want to live in a world where the white man is supposed to be superior. I want to be able to succeed without someone asking if I attend a "White School." I didn't know white people were the only ones subjected to a quality education. If people knew how ignorant they sound, I would hope they stop. I live in a world where I'm oppressed by my male counterpart daily. Where people don't believe the female gender is capable of running things. Where it's taken to the heart that I have the ability of having more power than a man. It just doesn't make sense.

My Skin
Kandise Hooks

My skin, which took me a while to love, is my
reason to embrace every flaw.
My skin, which took me a while to accept, is
my reason to forgive those who don't.
My skin, which set me back so many times, is
my reason to keep going and never look back.
My skin, which I learned to appreciate, is my
reason to not care about what others think.
My skin, which I ADORE,
My skin, which I LOVE,
My skin, which I ACCEPT,
My skin, which I APPRECIATE,
My skin, which IS ME,
Is my reason to stay BLACK and be what they
said I couldn't be!

Pops Gone
Mikeal Threatt

When I was little, I always wanted to see my pops. I heard everybody talk about how he was and where he was. But nobody would tell me where he really was. When I was about seven, my momma finally told me that he'd been in jail since before I was even born. When I first heard this, it didn't affect me but as I got older, the hurt set in and my behavior changed. I started to do things out of the ordinary. I used to rob, hit licks and was always fighting. I basically grew up without a pops. I didn't look at my step dad as a father figure until recently. We used to always fight cause I had the mindset that nobody could boss me around. I never told anybody about that though and it caused me to be more violent. Then I heard my dad was getting out of jail and I was happy. I was even thinking about moving in with him. Then I meet up my father, and the next thing I know my moms said I couldn't go over his house or see him anymore. She basically told him to stay away. Then my pops died. I really felt the pain of not having a father figure in my life. I finally got a chance to see my pops then a week later, he was dead. His own brother set him up, he got jumped and shot. My sister texted me and said daddy was gone. My heart was broke. I couldn't bear to think about it. Ever since then, my mindset been messed up. My trust been messed up. I've just really been messed up. I am not the type to express my feelings so I have been holding in so much pain. My head is forever messed up.

Typical Monday Morning
Eleonna Ware

I woke up on a Monday morning
wondering why I didn't go to school. My two
little cousins and I have been waiting for my
auntie to come get us. Nobody was in the house
but us when I woke up except my brothers. I
was so confused because usually I'd be at
school and usually my auntie would've picked
us up the night before. I got worried because
everyone was sugar coating things and wouldn't
answer my questions. My mom came in the
room and told my little cousins to get dressed. I
was wondering why she didn't tell me to get
dressed too. Everything was pissing me off and
I already figured something was really wrong.
After my cousins left, my brothers and I were
sitting in the room trying to figure out what was
going on. It was probably 15 minutes later my
auntie came in the room with tears in her eyes.
We're staring at her, waiting for her to say
something. "Your auntie got shot in the back of
her head last night," were the words that came
out of her mouth. A shower of tears started

falling down my face and not a peep of noise came out. That's when my life changed for the worse.

There is a girl trapped under a thin
veil of ice in dark, murky water
screaming at me to let her out.

I hear a voice….
"No."
She is my trauma.
I must set her free.

Wasn't Supposed to Be Normal
Diamond Jelks

My story begins with me having teen parents.
My Momma was only 14 and my Dad was 12.
So, yeah, it was pretty hard growing up. Couple
years after I was born, my parents split up. I
lived with my Grandma & Auntie. I have been
in and out of the hospital since I was born
because I have bad asthma and was a premature
baby (1 pound, 10 ounces). When I was born,
the doctors even told my mom that I would
never be normal. I wasn't supposed to walk,
talk or anything like a normal person. But now I
am 15 and doing everything they said I couldn't
and more. I currently live with my granny but
share an understanding bond with my mother
and not so much with my dad, he's pretty much
a part-time father. In 2014, I had a knife
incident that caused me to not have nerves in
my right thumb but I am here and I am blessed.

A Mother's Love
Sankeya Forrest

A mother has the gift of knowing when to hold, when to heal or when to help. A mother is a friend and when you have no one else, you have your mom. "Mama" is who you call when you need something. When you have a bad dream, "Mommy" is what you scream. "Maaaaa" when you are having boy problems. You lean on your mother when you think you are in love or when you have your first heartbreak. Ok "Ma" and a eye roll she gets when she tells you "no" and in return you get a slap to your face that makes you so angry. But you know inside that the handprint loves more than anything in the world. Mothers are there when your father says he is on his way but never comes or when he tells you he is coming to get you but then does not answer your phone call. Your mother is there to remind you that you are beautiful when you think different. So all we can do is thank them because there is no us without them.

Just Me?
Ericka Minor

I grew up going out of town a lot, like
different states. A lot of times for family events
with my auntie family. I haven't went out of
town with my mom but once, why? My mother
don't really associate with her family and plus
she's getting older. To be honest, I barely see
my mom's side of the family. Some of them
live away and barely any of them live in
Michigan. I mostly go out of town with my
auntie and uncle or when I'm with their son
Terrell or with his wife and his four kids.

I am an outgoing person but then I'm also
very shy. Like when I'm around my dad, I am
very shy. I be scared I'm going to say
something wrong. But can be the most friendly
and kind hearted person to anybody else. It's
just if it's my family or friends that I barely see
on a daily basis then imma be shy or I'm gone
seem awkward to them. I be like this around
people because I'm so use to being around
family that I see every day. Plus I be trying to
get help from teachers but I be so scared that I'll

say something wrong so I leave it alone. Then the next minute, I could really be trying to conversate with you. Crazy, I know right?

Basically, I'm hiding my feelings about things. I feel like you never know who you can trust. I've seen some of my family do people wrong so I felt I should do it as well. Feelings to me make me soft in my eyes because it's the truth that hurts. Plus, you don't want nobody to judge you about how you feel about anything or anybody. That's why you should just keep stuff to yourself sometimes, plus you don't need anybody in your business.

For Every Dark Night, There's a Brighter Day
Micah Barnes

Tupac once said "For every dark night, there's a brighter day." What if in those dark nights, you can't find your brighter days? What if in those brighter days there comes a darker night? What if those darker nights come even worse days? I want my darker nights to be brighter days and brighter days to be brighter nights, but you can't always get through a dark day with a fake and convincing smile. After so long when does enough become too much and when does too much become unbearable. That's why you put on that fake smile so no one knows the pain you really feel inside. Remember it has to rain before the sun can shine but what if it keeps raining and the sun never shines. What are you supposed to do? Who are you supposed to talk to?

That Type of Life
Deshawn Smith

Detroit born and raised in the hood where I
spent most of my days. In the hood was very
hard and difficult for my family because not a
lot of my family members had money. My mom
came along way and I still say to this day,
"MOM you came along way." As my mom
would say "yes we did, it was all cause of God."
With my parents being separated, it was very
hard for another man to try to step in and be my
dad. With my mom being so young, she had to
drop out of school to take care of me and my
brother. My mom would have to steal from
stores in order to put clothes on our back and
food in our mouths. My dad was also a young
person and couldn't do much for us. Had to
grind to get theirs, basically. But now my mom
is good and she doesn't need to steal anymore.
Guess what? My mom is now having a third
baby and she's so happy because of the fact she
doesn't need to steal from anyone and is
thankful she has the money to take care of the
child and so am I.

They Just Don't Know
Dante Belk

One day my friend kicked my other friend (they didn't know each other) and the friend that got kicked, pushed the other down and almost hit him. And it is only because my one friend was bullying everyone. Although I've never been bullied, I know that it is wrong, people don't like it and get depressed over it. Bullying is a serious problem and results in people being mean to each other. Most people say that bullying comes from problems at home but I believe that some people do it because they want to or it just comes to them. But sometimes it actually could be because they are being domestically abused. I see bullying happening everyday and people don't intentionally do it sometimes. When someone doesn't want another person to sit next to them because of their smell or how they look. They don't have to say anything to the person because that's unintentionally bullying someone. People just don't know what they are doing.

Broken Hearts
Silyce Lee

Saturday, January 28th, 2017 my life changed
for the worst. It was the middle of the night and
I was woke when my cousin decided to go out
to enjoy her night. She was out with her co-
worker friends having the time of her life.
When she decided to leave, she didn't feel like
driving home. So her friend did. The friend
wasn't doing the speed limit and hit a pothole on
the side of the street and the truck flipped up
and crashed. My cousin died instantly. Back at
the house I dozed off for about an hour and
woke back up and noticed she still wasn't back.
So I texted her phone and said "Mesha are you
ok? You've been gone for awhile" and I got no
reply. So I instantly got to worrying. A hour
later the police came to the door asking for her
husband and that he was needed at the hospital.
So at that time our hearts were going crazy.
Another hour later we called her husband and
asked "Was she ok?" but he paused and said
"I'll be there in a minute." Then he came
through the door and broke down saying "She

didn't make it!" My heart instantly fell apart and ever since that day, my heart remains the same and I smile and laugh everyday to keep from breaking down in front of everyone.

The Girl Behind The Mask
Janelle Boyles

You are probably wondering about that
one ordinary girl, the shy and tall ninth grader
with the slight smile that always makes her
friends laugh. She jokes around a lot, goofy,
teacher's favorite, a best friend you can lean on
when you're feeling blue, shy and very very
quiet. I know right, "Why is she so quiet all the
time, why do she stay to herself so much?" Well
little did everyone know that some people aren't
who they say they are or what mood they are in
behind those closed doors.

There's something she isn't telling us,
Well, this girl has been through a lot. She's
been through depression and suicidal attempts
at the age of eleven because she would always
get bullied in 6th grade about her face and how
skinny she was. No boy ever liked her and she
was always a loner and had no friends. Kids at
school would call her wart face, skinny stick
and many more mean things. She thought they
were just joking around but they'd always take

it too far. This girl never harmed anyone and she always stayed to herself.

In 7th grade I was a really outgoing girl and I was always so happy around my friends & family. Then March came by and that's when everything hit me. My grades started slipping, I grew in my depression and I had troubled relationships with my parents. My teen years were rough and that's when I decided to take all the pain away and thought maybe I should cut or kill myself. Even when I tried and tried and tried, the pain just wouldn't go away. There was a time when my mom had found out and she would try to take me to therapy but never did. There was a day when she called me weak because I guess if you're "Black" you can't have enough pain to kill yourself. But does race really define who you are and how much pain you can be in? I just don't get it.

The only person I could rely on was my grandmother and God, they were the only ones that will and are always gonna be there for me. It's kinda wrong for what I went through at such a young age. I really didn't deserve that, I was only 11. So if you're wondering why I always wear long sleeve shirts and put on a slight smile often now you know why. I use

those things to cover up the pain and hide the
girl behind this mask.

H.O.P.E (Hold On, Pain Ends)
Makayla Epps

Dear Future Self,

I just wanted to let you know that life is a circle of happiness, sadness, hard times and good times. If you are going through hard times, have faith, good times in our lives are on their way. Even though Auntie Marie is gone, don't forget what she told us. "Nunca es demasiado tarde para ser lo que padrias haber sido," meaning it's never too late to be what you might have been. There's one word I want you to live by and that's hope. I know what hope really means but our meaning is different. For us, H.O.P.E means Hold On, Pain Ends. We've been through a lot of physical and emotional pain. Heart breaks, people walking out on you and also finding the real reason why our father walked out on us. But no matter what, we can't let that break us or tear us apart. Yeah we cry a lot and get mad real fast but we're changing and forgetting what we did in the past. We're not letting people get the best of us anymore. Now have a good future, self.

Love,
Past Self

Growing Up in The "D"
Cher'maine Moreland

Growing up in the D,
With no shoes or you hungry.
In no gang,
Then you lonely.
And your enemy is the police.
Screw the Police!
They can't hold me.
White people, they don't know me.
I ain't gon let no enemy fold me.

Growing up in the D,
That's all I hear around me.
Gunshots, people screams.
Where young thugs are really kings and her hair
hangs to her knees.
This isn't the life Martin wanted for me.
When the police kills us,
Then we kill our own.
When your mother cries at night when she hears
the phone.

Growing up in the D,
A little blood don't scare me.
But I pray the hood spares me.

None of Yo Business
Cora Jarrell

My whole life, I've been told that stuff ain't
none of my business.

The people riding up and down my block at
night ain't none of my business, even though
when I look out my window at night I can see
them looking back at me, threatening to shoot
me down with just one look.

The screams I hear from across the street all the
time, at night and during the day, ain't none of
my business either because if it ain't got nothing
to do with me or if the screams I hear ain't
calling out my name then why should it matter
to me.

The reason my mama cries at night, thinking I
can't hear her sobs ain't my business, it's just the
bills and the stress of being a single mother
that's making her cry. Not the fact that once
we're black then we'll have a harder time at life
than anyone else. Not because my little brother

is making trouble at school and if he keeps on going like that then he's gonna end up dead or in jail. I'm a kid, why should I worry about the stress of being a parent if I ain't one.

The reason my daddy ain't want me or didn't think I was his child until now ain't my business either. Even though he left my mama to raise me by herself but why does that concern me. He was busy, he has 5 other kids that he had to take care of including his wife. I wasn't concerned with him so why should he be concerned with me?

The reason I get followed in stores ain't my business. They don't want a black kid in a hoodie walking around without being watched. It's for the safety of the store and the white people in it so if their only concerned about their customers safety then why should I be bothered.

The reason why my white friend always flinches when I raise my hand or pull something from my bag ain't my business. She's just shy and isn't used to black people wanting to be her friend or wanting to touch her. So if that's the case why should it matter to me.

Why people always ask me "Why did your mother name you Cora?" aint none of my business either. They're used to black girls having ghetto names that you can barely pronounce or spell. So if they got a reason, why should it matter.

They're just curious. Let them follow you around and let them talk about you like you can't hear. Let your teachers ask if you got private lessons or if you're mixed with something because "Wow!" you're so literate and can actually speak English. Let people in the street ask you to move from in front of their stores because they don't want no trouble. Let people look at you and ask if you are lost because this ain't the hood. Let them because for whatever reason it ain't yo business, even if it involves you.

Daddy Issues
Isis Brown

I have Daddy Issues. Yes, Isis Brown has
Daddy Issues. What I mean by "daddy issues"
is that I'm forever rejected by my father so I
look for another male to do the things I'm not
getting from my dad. I always talk to older guys
and sometimes they are very disrespectful or
even abuse or try to take advantage of me. I
didn't know any better. I thought those type of
things were okay and cute. I always thought
talking to older boys, they would treat me like
my dad was suppose to. I was wrong.

"We ask Black boys to become men without a childhood or a tear and wonder why they die so young."
- Howard Stevenson

From the Bahamas to Detroit
Lenardo Moss

I was born in the Bahamas where I spent my whole fifteen years at. I moved to Detroit Because I used to get in a lot of fights and had problems in school and my mom wanted to come over to the states to cool down and possibly change my ways. I came to Detroit in June and people talk way different than me. Some of their accents is very funny to me and they say I am the one with the accent.

This is my first time in the USA. Some of the people from Detroit said that I talk different and they like my accent and some of them try to speak just like me. But some of them ask me ridiculous questions like do you'll have malls in the Bahamas? Do you`ll eat bugs and rice? Sometimes I get mad because we don't eat bugs but we do eat rice. And they think Africa is just like the Bahamas but I have to remember that most of them have never been to the Bahamas so they will ask ignorant things like that because they just don't know.

I still don't know which one I like better, Detroit or the Bahamas. I have to see more things in Detroit that I've never seen before to tell if it's better than the Bahamas. Sometimes I miss the Bahamas because some of my friends are there and I miss them but I have great memories of them and am grateful to now be in Detroit.

Unequaled
Mariah Mangum

They say I'm not the average black girl because
I'm so well spoken as a white man's token.

You know I remember when Shakira told me
that being black is a natural beauty in me.
I didn't know how I was gonna react when I
was brought around different colored people
because I knew how they would talk behind my
back but it taught me so very well that being
black could never break you.

They say I'm not the average black girl.

Not the average black girl because the pigment
of my skin is just a shade darker than that black
girl over there.
You know, the black girl over there,
The black girl with the nappy hair.

Whose hearts and heads are filled up with self-
hate and bottled up emotion.

The cocoa brown girls who have to face society
every day and be tough,
Because no matter how good they straighten
their hair, their good is still not good enough

Oh, but see. Luckily for me, see
I don't fall in that category.

See they say I'm not the average black girl
because I speak with so much class and
I don't have too much but just enough
pizzazz.
You know, just a little bit of attitude.
Cause you don't wanna come off as rude.
You know, popping their gum and rolling their
neck.
Yeah, 'cause those black girls get little to no
respect.
But see luckily for me, see I get a pass.
'Cause the melanin in my skin matches that
brown paper bag.
And my father, brother and men that I date
don't sag.
Growing up in the suburbs for me, being the
average black girl, I saw a lot.

My trials and tribulations of being the average black girl helped me become who I am now, Unequaled to others.

Growing Up Without
Mya Percy

Growing up without a father is very hard. No one to tell you that you're their little princess. No one to call daddy. No one to talk to you when mom is not around. Not knowing how a men should treat you cause you never had a father to show you. Not knowing that if he came back, how things would be. Everything would be okay. We would be a family. But would I even like him? Would I love him? No there's no way I would ever forgive him. He wasn't there when I was growing up and I knew it would never be the same. Growing up without a father is the reason I can't love properly.

See You in The Clouds
Leondre Houston

My uncle had cancer. His favorite color was
pink. So much stuff on my mind it's hard for
me to think. I'm at that point where I could
really use a drink. It's funny how you had to die
to make the whole family link. I saw you laying
and that brought tears to my eyes. I told my
momma that I love her every time she got us by.
It's crazy how we come together every time
someone die. I pulled your picture from my
wallet and put it up to the sky. You died before
I could even show you the promise I made to
you. I'm going to be a better dad because of
you. You were there when it was daddy day
visits in class. Lots of memories and I try to put
them in the past. It's ok. I cried when I saw you
in that suit. You are legendary in my eyes. You
even told me the truth when I made it to the
hospital room. Your cancer was stage two. I
remember I was home when I first got that call.
That hit me so hard that I was crying out for
you. I felt like I had lost a fight. So I just threw

in the towel. This all happened in four straight
months. See you in the clouds.

Voice Trapped In Silence
Earneasha Byars

She was silence in a world so loud.
Voice trapped like rain within a cloud.
Is it true that even the smallest voices are
heard?
But when she speaks they don't seem to hear a
word.
Pain is temporary they say.
Then how come I feel it every day?
They want my joy, they want my pride.
Some things I let slip, maybe even ride.
I wonder if they'll ever hear me.
Will this trapped voice ever be free?
She was silence in a world so loud.
If only they knew she was crying out loud.

The Struggle

From the age of 7, I have been called every name in the book. Gay, bitch, fag, stupid, etc. It's all because I am a homosexual male, because I'm not like the other kids in the school. In the second grade people would hit me and beat me up because I'm different. I have never liked violence but when you grow up in a drug filled neighborhood and a drug filled household, then that's really all you know. I remember my stepdad used to beat on me because he found out I liked the same sex. He used to tell me that "you not shit, you not gone be shit." It used to hurt me because how can you talk about a child, hurt them and not care? It's so hard for me to even talk about this situation, to this day.

In the third grade, I was raped by a white man. He offered me a drink because I had to walk a long way home. I went to the house and he told me to come in and close the door. I got kinda nervous so I just walked away. Then he grabbed my arm and pulled me into the house. He pulled me to a dark room that had nothing but a lamp in it and a bed. The bed had red blood stains on it. The whole time this was happening, I was screaming and he said "There's no point in screaming, I don't have any neighbors so no one can hear you anyways." I didn't care what he said, I kept screaming and kicking. Then he started to take off my clothes. I really had no clue what was happening and that's how I turned gay. So when I found out and accepted it, my whole world changed.

One time a kid threw a chair at me because he said that a kid told him that I had a crush on him. He threw the chair and then I had to get rushed to the hospital. I hated it at the hospital. Always trying to drug me up or give me some type of shot. While I was in the hospital my mom only came around a few times. The first time she came she asked me why did we fight. I didn't tell her the real reason we fought, I told her that he punched me, I got mad and punched him back then he threw the chair at me. After those words, she went back home and I had to stay in the hospital for 1 to 2 more weeks. My cousins came and seen me more than my mom did. They came almost everyday which meant a lot to me.

In the fifth grade, I had a racist teacher. He

failed me because I was black and called my mom for every little thing and at the end of the school year he called me a "Gay little black boy." I didn't know what to do except cry about it. I felt so many things that day. Sad, unloved, scared, lonely, but most of all betrayed. I felt betrayed most of all because I thought that a teacher was supposed to care for you no matter what. Even if they didn't like you, they should at least keep their words to their self. I never told my mom about that either. I never told her anything because I thought that she would never love me because I liked the same sex and it would hurt me that my mom doesn't love me because of my sexuality. In the seventh grade, I got bullied by the whole school except for the girls. I was very bullied by one particular boy in the 8th grade.

One day I was walking home with two of my friends when the boy tripped me then he jumped on top of me and started to punch me over and over again. He finally stopped and afterwards, I walked up to "my friends" and asked "Why didn't yall help me?" They told me that "They didn't care if I got beat up or not." I basically found out the hard way that everyone isn't your real friend. I really felt betrayed on that day and now that's why I don't have as many friends as I'd like.

That same year, I got back in contact with my bestfriend that I have known for nine years. I was so happy, my whole world changed. I never told her about me being gay either so I told her and how it happened. She told me that she already knew and that it was okay. One day, me and my bestfriend had a long conversation and she told me that I should come out to everyone and my mom and then people would respect me a little more. I kept telling her no but she ended up talking me into it anyway.

A few weeks after that my mom and my stepdad got into a big fight. They got into a fight because my stepdad was cheating on my mom. My mom was in the house with me, my sister, and my brother. My step dad was outside with a gun and and all you could hear is my mom and stepdad yelling back and forth. Then one gun shot fired "BANG" then another "BANG." I was super scared and I thought my sister got shot but she was just crying cause she was scared. So one of the people that lived on that block called the cops. He got sent to jail for having an unlicensed gun and firing it.

It was that same summer my mom cussed

me out because she started to notice my mannerisms and saw me wearing a rainbow bandana. When she seen it, she asked me about it. I told her that the bandana was my bestfriend's and I forgot that I had it on. Then she said, "Nigga you need to tell me something cause I don't want no gay ass son." I snatched the bandana off my head and walked into the house. The next day I told my bestfriend what happened. She got super mad but I told her not to worry about it but she was still upset and concerned.

After the first month of summer, I had to live with my grandmother. She treated me like a dog off the street. She used to tell me that I was dumb and didn't know anything. It used to hurt me because she was the one to tell my mom to keep me because my mom found out that she was going to have me after being raped by a man when she was 14 years old. But me and my mom got back in contact over Facebook because my grandmom wouldn't let my mom see me. So when I found her, I ran away with her.

It was three weeks after that, that my mother started to dog me out again. And it was only because my new stepdad was beating on her.

One day they got into a big fight and my new stepdad was on top of my mom hitting her in the face. I had to watch my mom get beat. But something told me "You can't watch this, you have to do something." So my first thought was to go straight up and fight him but no, so I went to the kitchen grabbed a knife and cut him in the back. He fell down and I got up, grabbed my mom and my brother and we left. It was the middle of the night so we really didn't have anywhere to go but to an abandoned house.

My little sister and my first youngest brother were in Ohio. With their dad or grandparents I should say. They have been there ever since their dad got out of jail. Then he got put back in jail because he got caught drunk driving and he had drugs in the car. Me and my mom have been fighting to get them back ever since we got separated and it has been a real challenge.

I remember one day I was at my Godmom's house and she asked me if I wanted to go to Chicago with her. I said yeah and we ended up leaving the very next night. It was so beautiful. My Godaunt is a professor at Judson University and I had an opportunity to talk about my life. I told the class the 5 times I had to go to foster care. And everytime I went I got beat. One time one of the ladies threw a heel at me and that's why I have this mark on the corner of my left eye. One girl in the class asked me "If you were able to change one thing in your life, what would it be?" which I replied, "Nothing, because I know that God is putting me through the struggle for a reason and it made me the person I am today." After that, everyone started to clap and started crying. This day is so special to me because it landed on April 2nd which is my birthday and that is a memory that I will cherish for the rest of my life.

Then the day came when my mom finally found out that I was gay. She found out because I was writing a poem to my boyfriend and I left it on the kitchen table. When I was going to the bathroom I wasn't paying it any mind and she was going to the kitchen. As soon as I got into the bathroom, I finally realized that I left it there. I stayed in the bathroom terrified about what she would say or even do. When I came out the bathroom the first thing she said was "What the fuck is this?" I said the first lie that came to mind. "Oh, that's for one of my friends, she said she wanted me to write it for her." She slapped me and said "NO NIGGA! YO NAME IS IN THIS!" At this time, I could feel the heat coming from her body and her face was blood red. I sat down and started to cry. "Mom I'm gay and the boy's name that's in there is my boyfriend." She told me straight to my face "I hate you and want nothing to do with you." I looked at her like she was one of the kids that talked about me in school. I couldn't believe she said that to me. Do you know how it feels for your mom to say that she hates you? It feels like someone you love is shooting you a million times. And at the same time not knowing who my real dad is or feeling like I was supposed to be an accident. Hearing my mom saying that hurt me. Afterwards, she tried to change me instantly. She tried to make me watch porn and videos on how gay people get diseases. She even told me that because I'm gay that I'm going to hell. Well I felt like I was already there because of what she put me through. After that, I distanced myself from everyone and didn't eat for about two months. My mom didn't care though, she only cared if I was straight or not. She would ask atleast twice a week if I was still gay or not. The third month I guess she finally accepted it.

Everyday I would go to school with makeup and girl clothes on and my mom never knew.

When it was time to go home I would change clothes and take off all the make-up. Basically when I had to take it all off, I felt like it was a costume to me. Even though it hurt me, I'm still here on this Earth. My lived experiences still hurt but it means nothing to me because I am powerful and I know that I have a purpose on this Earth. Yall words can't hurt me anymore. And yall still gone see me wearing what I want and saying "Hey girl" and "Bye Felicia!" And it's all because I can and because I want to. You have to understand that there are kids out there killing themselves because of kids that are talking about them.

When I was younger, I used to scratch my forehead until it started to bleed because I thought I was able to get the thoughts of people talking about me outta my head. I would try to overdose on pills and everything. When I went to school, I would have to wear hats to cover my head so no one would see the bruises. One day my teacher told me to take off the hat and when I did I got sent to foster care because she thought that my mom was beating on me. So if you don't understand what I'm trying to say to you then oh' well. But just know that your words can't hurt me anymore cause I'm stronger

than you think I am and I'm never going to
stoop down to your level. I've been through way
too much for those words to hurt me. Please
don't judge me, just try to understand my
struggle.

"Your trauma is valid. Even if other people have experienced "worse." Even if someone else who went through the same experience doesn't feel debilitated by it. Even if it "could have been avoided." Even if it happened a long time ago. Even if no one knows. Your trauma is real and valid and you deserve a space to talk about it. It isn't desperate or pathetic or attention-seeking. It's self-care. It's inconceivably brave. And regardless of the magnitude of your struggle, you're allowed to take care of yourself by processing and unloading some of the pain you carry. Your pain matters. Your experience matters. And your healing matters. Nothing and no one can take that away."

- Daniell Koepke

Healing Mantra

I see the promise and potential my future holds!
I accept my situation, I am where I am and I can build on that!
I have a bright future!
I give my body love and space to heal!
I am grateful to my body for everything it does to support me!
I am still standing!
I am reassured!
I am safe!
I am loved and supported!
Fear contracts, love expands. I allow myself to relax, to feel love and to expand!
I am worthy!
I am reassured and safe!
My self-esteem and confidence are growing!
I move forward and leave the past behind with confidence!
I can do this!
I am peace!
I am love!
All is Well!

Acknowledgements

Thank you to our moms, dads, siblings and family members who have encouraged us and loved us. Thank you to Principal Bell who inundated us with his laugh and taught us that our characters are just as important as our academics. Thank you to Mrs. Crudup for teaching us how to solve our own problems and to always look at ourselves first...constant self-reflection and humility. Thank you to Mrs. Asberry for having her character preach more loudly than her words and showing us why math matters. Thank you to Ms. Murrell for never giving up on us and showing us daily that we are efficient. Thank you to Mr. Lewis for always keeping it real and for letting us release our great levels of energy in gym class. Thank you to Mrs. Lee for teaching us that we need to know our history to better our futures and for showing us how to navigate difficult situations. Thank you to Ms. Hickey for showing us the real meaning of empathy and prepping us to be future world-renowned chefs. Thank you to Ms. Greer for the warm reminders, kindness and compassion. Thank you to Mr. Lewis for having a heart made of gold and for keeping our school home together and safe. To the entire city of Detroit, thank you!

Peace & Love,
DC Scholars

"Silence is not the price you have to pay for your survival anymore. Speak. Scream. Roar."

- Nikita Hill